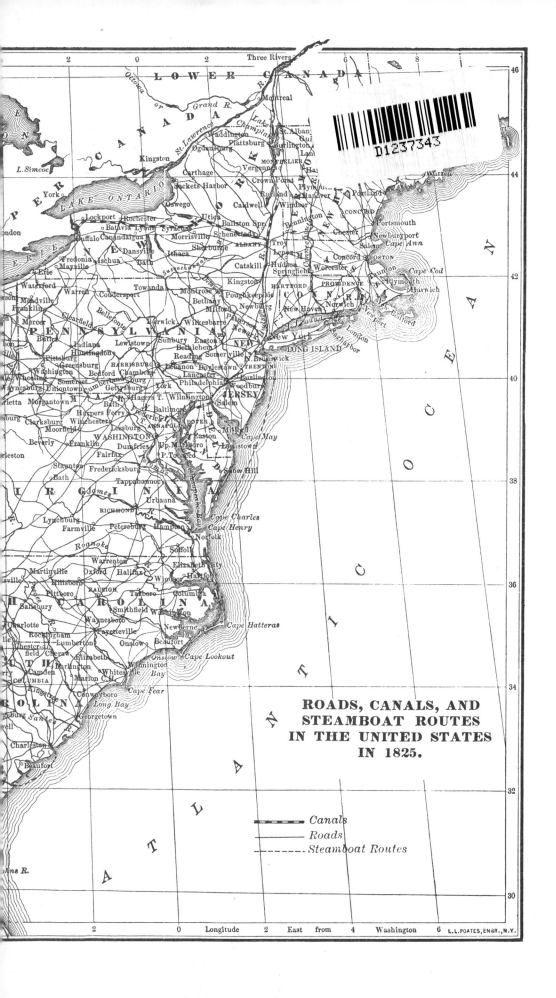

ROADS, CANALS, AND
STEAMBOAT ROUTES
IN THE UNITED STATES
IN 1825.

Canals
Roads
Steamboat Routes

Only 650 copies of
this book were printed.
This is Number **401**

The
OVERLAND
EXPRESS

By William H. Rideing.

Being a Correct True Account of Earliest
Beginnings in *NEW ENGLAND*, battlefront
service during the Civil War & perilous
Adventures in the *FAR WEST*, 1837–1875.

INTRODUCTION by Richard Dillon.

ASHLAND
LEWIS OSBORNE
1970

SBN 87767-000-5

INTRODUCTION

THANKS TO THE MANY romantic accounts of the Pony Express and to entire shelves of books about Wells, Fargo, a name which has become virtually synonymous with the word express, the literature of the express business in America is large and growing.

But this is a rather recent publishing phenomenon, a by-product of the booming "industry" of Western Americana and, curiously, the historical background of this most interesting aspect of American commerce is not well-known. There are several reasons for this. First, there are few early books to be found on the subject and, indeed, fewer still which cover the entire history of the business from its founding. Second, there is a confusion over just what the word express implies. Many books are more concerned with such peripheral matters as stagecoaching and the skill of jehus like Hank Monk or road agents like Black Bart than they are with the express, *per se*. The word does not mean staging or freighting any more than it signifies banking or the Overland Mail, although it is hard to segregate these parallel and related matters in the Far West where the distinctions were particularly blurred even without Wells, Fargo's delivering the U.S. Mail and dominating such transportation companies as the Pioneer Stage Line of Hangtown-to-Carson City fame.

By dictionary definition, an express company is a firm which engages in the rapid transportation of merchandise and which provides special care and security as well as fast delivery. It can choose to do this via paddlewheel steamer, railroad car or Model T. But, of course, it was the combination of the Concord coach and "treasure"—specie, bullion or gold dust, rather than mere goods or merchandise— which seized the imagination of readers.

The express business not only grew enormously along with the West but largely on account of the West, with its desperate need for communications with the States. However, it was not born during the Gold Rush but, rather, a decade earlier in the East. The origins and general pre-El Dorado years of this strictly American business invention are little-known even to avid readers of American history, because practically no major book appeared from publishers' row between A. L. Stimson's pioneering effort of 1858, *History of the Express Business* . . . , and the classic collector's item of 1934, Alvin F. Harlow's *Old Waybills*. The latter title triggered a still ongoing editorial explosion which saw the brief Pony Express story told and retold by authors like Roy Bloss and Ralph Moody, and the Wells, Fargo saga sung by Winther, Wilson, Beebe, Hungerford, Jackson and Dillon. Even the American Express Company finally got one book, Alden Hatch's 1950 *American Express*.

True, there were books between Stimson and Harlow, but who has ever heard of W. N. Chandler's (1914) *The Express Service and its Rates* or Bertram Benedict's (1919) *The Express Companies of the United States?* Stimson's volume went through three editions by 1881, but still it was necessary to tell the story of the express business to the public in general. This was done by lectures, pamphlets and periodical articles, the ephemera so desired by collectors today. Here one finds such rare works as the Albany imprints of Henry Wells himself, *The American Express in its Relation to the City of Buffalo* (1863) and *Sketch of the Rise, Progress and Present Condition of the Express System* (1864). Standing with these is the major early magazine essay on the subject, "An American Enterprise," which appeared without by-line in the August 1875 number of *Harper's New Monthly Magazine* and which is reprinted here for the first time.

This account of the history of the express forwarding business was not composed by someone in the business, like Wells, but by one of *Harper's* most dependable and skilled professional writers, William H. Rideing. This essayist was a popularizer, to be sure, who could discuss both Staten Island and the South Sea Islands and write as easily about the Wheeler Survey as about The Old Lady of Threadneedle Street. He was a prodigious and prolific writer, out-articling even J. Ross Browne (thirty-five to nineteen) according to the index to the first seventy volumes of *Harper's*. But he was not a mere hack, a Yankee Grub-Streeter. Rideing was one of America's most talented freelance writers of the 19th Century, a lesser Bayard Taylor, although he is completely forgotten today.

Born in Liverpool of a seafaring family on February 17, 1853, Rideing was well educated in private schools but was orphaned at sixteen years old. Instead of going to sea, he migrated to a point in the United States about as far from salt water as possible—Chicago, Illinois. He was determined to live by the pen after a Liverpool paper published a work of fiction by him, and thanks to an admirable apprenticeship, Rideing succeeded in his aspiration. On the strength of his letter of application which displayed good sense as well as superb penmanship, Samuel Bowles of the prestigious *Springfield Republican* hired Rideing as his private secretary. He later worked for the *Newark Journal*, the *Boston Journal* and Whitelaw Reid's *New York Tribune* as a kind of utility journalist, a jack of all treatises, contributing material on a wide variety of subjects until he saw the possibility of becoming a genuine freelance or, as he himself put it, "a handy man of literature."

Rideing gave up newspaper writing, except for a special *New York Times* assignment as special correspondent with the Wheeler Survey in the West (which produced articles and the books *A-Saddle in the Far West* and *Pacific Railways Illustrated*) and from 1874 until his death at his home, Brandon Hall, in Brookline, Massachussetts, on August 22, 1918, he was a major contributor to such magazines as *Harper's*, *Scribner's* and *Book News Monthly*, sometimes working with such renowned illustrators as Howard Pyle or

Edwin A. Abbey and occasionally traveling as far as his native England in search of a story. Although he eventually wrote fifteen books of travel, biography, reminiscence and fiction for both adults and young people, including *In the Land of Lorna Doone*, *The Boyhood of Living Authors*, *Many Celebrities*, *Thackeray's London*, *At Hawarden With Mr. Gladstone* and *Young Folks' History of London*, he became best-known in his day as an editor on the staffs of the *North American Review*, the *Youth's Companion* and (in London) *Dramatic Notes*. Although the talented Liverpudlian was short in stature, he bore himself with the dignity befitting a friend and confidant of such celebrities as Cardinal Manning, William Makepeace Thackeray, Alfred Lord Tennyson, Prime Minister William Gladstone and the great American iconoclast, Robert Ingersoll.

Compilers of biographical dictionaries have found it difficult to pin-point Rideing's profession. To *Appleton's Cyclopedia of Biography* he was an author; to *Who's Who in America* he was an editor. Toronto University Librarian W. Stewart Wallace found him to be a journalist in his *Dictionary of North American Authors*. The *Dictionary of American Biography* described him as both writer and editor. Perhaps Stanley Kunitz and Howard Haycraft put it best in their *American Authors, 1600–1900* by defining him as an "editor and miscellaneous writer." None, alas, chose to give him the title of essayist, to elevate him to the company of Addison or Emerson, but, on the other hand, none wrote him off as a humble hack, producing pot-boilers merely to feed himself and his wife, Margaret.

In any case, Rideing was a good choice for the task of summarizing the history of the express business for the general public. A talented writer of non-fiction, he was familiar with William F. Harnden's origination of express-forwarding between his own Boston and New York.

Rideing perhaps exaggerated a little when he wrote that the express business surpassed all private enterprises in the world with the exception of the railroads and telegraphs. *Harper's* (encouraged by Rideing) claimed that the business had created fifteen American millionaires by 1875. But certainly the express business was as American a contribution to civilization as, say, the public library or apple pie, and was the Yankee equivalent of Britain's 19th-century leadership in banking. Rideing was one of the first to be struck by the phenomenon of express routes which, already in 1875, webbed the continent as the result of Harnden's gamble—the purchase of a carpet bag in 1837 to transport other people's papers and goods from New York to Boston by steamboat and railroad.

As Rideing explains in his essay, Harnden afterward allowed himself to become distracted by emigration schemes, and leadership of the express business passed first to his rival, Alvin Adams of Adams Express Company, and thence to Henry Wells and William Fargo, whose names remain household words today. Wells, as Harnden's agent in Albany in 1841, urged his boss to extend his express lines to the West. According to Rideing, Harnden's answer was: "Put a people there and my express shall follow." Wells, in his own writings, had Harnden speaking even more bluntly (and short-sightedly): "If *you* choose to run an express to the Rocky Mountains, you had better do it on your own account. *I* choose to run an express where there is business." Wells believed it was the other way around; put out lines of communication in the West and the population—and profits—would follow. He started in 1842 by carrying oysters on his Western Express Line from Albany to Buffalo at $3.00 per hundred—per hundred *bivalves*, not per hundred*weight*. By 1850, with the help of Fargo, he was able to throw a scare into the monopoly of the Adams Express Company by forming the American Express Company. They compounded the shock in 1852 by carving the continent in half, like Spain and Portugal divvying up the world at Tordesillas in 1494. The eastern United States was to be the territory of the parent company but the land west of the Mississippi was to be the domain of the newborn Wells, Fargo & Company, son of American Express. This was the plan, although Adams had pioneered a California express as early as 1849. Wells wrote, "An attempt to establish another company in the face of their formidable opposition and acquired influence demanded much courage and determination." But by 1854 depression-wracked Adams & Company was ready to call it quits in California, leaving the Golden State to Wells, Fargo.

According to Lucius Beebe, Wells, Fargo was earning $12,000,000 per year in Nevada freight charges alone by 1864, when it had 156 agencies scattered over the map of the West. Two years before Rideing wrote his article, Wells, Fargo had had to hire ex-El Dorado County Sheriff James B. Hume to be its chief of detectives, as bandits made war on the drivers of stages carrying the firm's sturdy green treasure-express boxes.

As the package express service metamorphosed into the transport of riches in the Far West, there was created a parasitic big business in crime. Jim Hume, compiling a *Robbers Report* for Wells, Fargo in the 1880's, found that in fourteen years bandits had carried out 346 stage holdups, all but thirty-three of them successful, and eight train heists of which half were successful. The Company lost $415,312.55, plus the lives of two Wells, Fargo messengers, four drivers and four passengers, in addition to having a number of persons wounded by bandits. But in that time Hume and his associates disposed of seventeen road agents (*permanently*) and secured convictions of 226 stage or train robbers who managed to survive the attentions of his shotgun messengers and deputized posse men.

—Richard H. Dillon

TRAVELLERS on the Long Island Sound of about thirty-seven years ago* might have observed on board the steamer then running between Providence and New York an under-sized, delicately built, sanguine-looking young man, who accompanied the vessel on alternate trips, and constantly carried in his hand a small carpet-bag of half a bushel capacity. He was William F. Harnden, and his bag contained the beginnings of the express forwarding business of the United States, which, with the exception of the railways and telegraphs, now surpasses all other private enterprises in the world.

Born at Reading, Massachusetts, in 1812, he was employed as conductor of the first passenger train that ran in New England, and was afterward promoted to the position of ticket agent on the Boston and Worcester Railway. The sedentary desk-work did not suit him, however, and in 1837 he came to New York in search of more congenial employment. At the corner of Wall and Pearl streets stood the old Tontine Coffee-house, a famous resort for the merchants and ship-owners of those days, and in connection with it there was an admirable newsroom—a sort of Lloyd's or Garraway's—conducted by James W. Hale, a local celebrity, who afterward extended his fame by promoting a cheap postal system in opposition to the government. Mr. Hale was a man of varied experience and a genial disposition. He was one of the most active men of his day, and Harnden went to him for advice in seeking employment. Hale became interested in him, and in the course of a few days advised him to establish himself as an expressman between New York and Boston—a business never before transacted and a name never before assumed.

As there have been other claimants to the honor of having originated the enterprise, and as Mr. Hale is still living, I will repeat a statement which he made to me in July last.

---

*I.e., 1838. The reader is reminded that this account was written in 1875.

There was never a day, he said, that inquiries were not made at the news-room for some person going to Boston or Providence. Some wanted to send small parcels to their friends, others letters or circulars; but the most frequent applicants were money-brokers, who wanted to forward packages of Eastern bank-notes to Boston for redemption. If an acquaintance was found on the boat, he was pounced upon without ceremony, and burdened with the packages, which were sometimes worth many thousand dollars. But if a friend did not appear, the things were often intrusted to entire strangers, with the modest request that they would deliver them immediately after their arrival. Merchants and brokers seeking gratuitous transportation for their letters contributed largely to the excitement attending the departure of the steamer, and many persons will remember the nights of anxiety they have passed on the Sound, when such unexpected wealth has been temporarily thrust upon them. "When Harnden called upon me for advice," Mr. Hale stated, "I thought of the daily inquiries made at my office, 'Do you know any body going to Boston this evening?' and I immediately advised him to travel between the two cities and do errands for the business men. I also suggested that the new enterprise should be called 'The Express,' which gave the idea of speed, promptitude, and fidelity."

Harnden hesitated for several days, doubting whether the scheme would be profitable, but eventually he decided to try it, and bought the historic traveling-bag, which is still preserved in Boston. A small slate for orders was hung in the news-room, and the patrons of that institution were Harnden's chief patrons. The old merchants had become so accustomed to transportation of smaller articles without cost that they did not readily observe the advantages "the express" offered, and at the end of two months Harnden found all his capital absorbed. His receipts were less than his expenses, and he would have discontinued the service had not some friends procured free passages for him on an

WILLIAM F. HARNDEN.

opposition steamboat. With the passage-money as a sub-
sidy, "the express" prospered, and the business so increased
that Harnden soon engaged an assistant.

Goods were forwarded every evening instead of three times a week, and the carpet-bag was successively multiplied by two and three, until in the flush of prosperity a large trunk was bought, which in turn was substituted by a yet larger one.

Harnden next disposed of an interest in the concern to his oldest assistant, Dexter Brigham, and opened two offices—one in Boston, which he occupied himself, and the other in New York, which he left in charge of his partner. Two men were hired to follow the goods on the route, and a small hand-car or crate was placed on board each steamer. "The express" had surmounted the worst obstacles, and its utility was clearly demonstrated. The receipts gradually increased, and Harnden's heart beat fast one night as he counted by candle-light in his dusty office the magnificent

LEAVING NEW CHURCH STREET, NEW YORK, ON THE MORNING RUN.

BROADWAY, NEW YORK, IN 1875.

amount of twenty dollars earned in a single day! But his success was the result of unceasing overwork, which undermined his constitution, and often caused him to say that he would not live to reap the full harvest. A. L. Stimpson, an old expressman, states that his endurance was a subject of wonder to all who knew him, and that it was only by an almost superhuman exertion of will that he sustained his exhausted system and discharged his recurring labors. An indomitable spirit stimulated him, and he bravely encountered the vicissitudes of his business at all times, often against the remonstrances of friends. Among other things, it was his pride to be first in boarding the Cunard steamers to obtain news for the press; and even though the arrival was after midnight, he and his men were invariably on the alert.

It was the opening of the Cunard service between Liverpool and Boston that did most for his express, by which all valuable parcels from Europe for New York were forwarded; and it was the Cunard steamers that aroused the greatest aspirations in his breast. His acquaintances constantly urged him to extend his business westward, and he so far followed their advice as to establish the route between Boston and Albany. He would not go farther in that direction, however, as he thought it a waste of time to court the patronage of the unpopulated prairies. "Put a people there," he said to Henry Wells, who afterward became a principal in the celebrated house of Wells, Fargo, and Co., "and my express shall soon follow." The idea presented to him was retained in his memory, nevertheless, and before long it resolved itself into an extraordinary colonization project. In brief, Harnden decided to make an opening for a lucrative express business in the West by filling it himself with a thrifty people. He was fairly infatuated with the scheme, into which he entered with greater zeal than ever. Night and day it occupied his thoughts. His pale face became a shade paler, and his fragile body a degree thinner under the intense excitement wrought. It seemed to offer princely wealth, unexampled honor and power. All his resources were expended upon it, and in 1841 the "English and Continental Express" was established, with offices in Liverpool, London, and Paris.

Hitherto there had been no organized system of emigration. The emigrants already settled here had no safe and economical means of remitting money to or prepaying the passage of their relations across the water. Harnden began by supplying the want. Branch offices were opened in nearly all the large towns of Germany, France, and Great Britain for the payment of bills of exchange purchased by persons in the United States in favor of those left behind in the older countries. The arrangement was widely advertised, and Irish and German residents in America availed themselves of it to such an extent that the increased emigration was very noticeable. But it was only a small part of the complete

HENRY WELLS.

scheme. Harnden next contracted with the owners of a line
of sailing vessels for the cheap conveyance of emigrants
from Liverpool, and chartered a considerable fleet of Erie
Canal passenger boats. It was his design to have every emi-
grant arriving in Boston or New York ticketed to the firm
of Harnden and Co. In a very short time he had almost succeeded in controlling the traffic, and it is to his credit that
he never took any unfair advantage the monopoly offered.
Those laborers whom he brought here were protected from

swindlers in the sea-board cities, and forwarded with as much speed and comfort as possible to the agricultural districts of the West. "Within three years of the inception of the enterprise," writes A. L. Stimpson, to whom we allude for the last time, with thanks for the service he has been to us, "that small-sized, fragile man, whose constitution was now broken down by the consumption which was rapidly measuring the little remnant of life yet left to him, had the satisfaction of knowing that he had been the direct means of bringing from the Old World more than one hundred thousand hard-handed laborers, and depositing them in that now magnificent portion of our country where their work was most wanted for the cultivation of the soil and the construction of railways and canals."

Vast as it was its in operations, the colonization venture did not pay. Harnden was too lavish and magnificent in all his dealings. He paid his employés large salaries, and advertised with the greatest liberality. He understood the value of publicity, and in the earliest days of his career he exerted himself to serve the newspapers. Thanks to Harnden for the prompt delivery of packages were often found in the Boston *Transcript*, with many a kindly word of commendation added. A clerk of his was once told to order some advertising cards. Harnden afterward inquired from the printer what kind of cards had been chosen, and was informed that the order given by the clerk was for a thousand, white in color, and about the size of his hand.

"His hand!" Harnden exclaimed. "Have them a foot square, five thousand of them, and the color red. If a thing's worth doing at all, it's worth doing thoroughly."

During the winter of 1844 his health failed him completely, and he sought relief in the South. The skill of the best physicians could not save him, and he died on January 14, 1845, a poor man.

The Harnden Express was in its earliest stage when a young Vermonter, Alvin Adams by name, engaged in the

A view of Omaha, Nebraska, in 1875.

produce business at Boston, became much impressed with
its utility and prospects. He had little capital and no influ-
ential supporters. Health, energy, and industry were his
principal possessions. While he was thinking of Harnden's
future and wishing that his own were as bright, the little
money he had was lost by a sudden fluctuation in the produce market, and he had to begin again at the lowest round
of the ladder. He had no taste for his old trade, and he resolved to start an opposition express. It was a difficult task
that he had chosen, and for several months there seemed to
be no prospect that he would ever make any progress. He
was considered an interloper on Harnden's ground, and

many persons openly refused to patronize him. Even his own friends "damned him with faint praise," and the partner who joined him at the outset soon retired in despair. He was his own messenger, cashier, clerk, label boy, and porter. All the parcels intrusted to him might have been carried in his hat. A wagon or a horse was not to be thought of, and the entire "establishment" consisted of Adams, a valise, and desk room in an office. The year, too, was a most unfavorable one for all new enterprises, as the mercantile interests of the community were in an inactive and ominous condition. Adams had to encounter, therefore, not only the disadvantages of a poor beginner, but also the antagonism of those with whom he had to deal and the trade depression of an inauspicious time. For three long years he toiled with little or no encouragement. It is unfair to contrast the two men, perhaps, but we can not help thinking Adams the superior of Harnden in courage and steadfast faith. Several times the latter was disheartened and nearly succumbing, but his rival, whose circumstances were much poorer, never for a moment thought of surrender, and worked with heroic perseverance through thirty-six months of the bitterest experiences. We can think of few other such examples for struggling young men. No doubt he was sustained by his confidence in the worth of his object in life, but that fact redounds still more to his credit.

We have mentioned that Harnden and Co. became so engrossed with the extension of the emigration venture that the home express was neglected, and Adams thus got a chance that otherwise he might never have had. Parcels were often delayed by the Harnden Express, and after a while some of its best customers began to transfer considerable patronage to Adams. In the meantime the latter had entered into a partnership with Ephraim Farnsworth, who subsequently retired, and was succeeded by William B. Dinsmore, who worked for scarcely enough to pay his board bill, sharing his superior's confidence in the ultimate

ALVIN ADAMS.

success of the concern. Adams and Co. then employed two
men and a boy, and it was a difficult matter to make both
ends meet. The driver of their delivery and collecting wagon
was "Old Sam Woodward," formerly a stage-coach driver,
who possessed in no ordinary measure that humorous loqua-
city for which his tribe were famed. In soliciting freight from
the merchants he brought all his eloquence to bear, with the
greatest success. Seeing a box or parcel at the door of some
store waiting for Harnden's Express, he would dismount
from his wagon and expatiate on the inestimable benefits of

forwarding the goods by the Adams line. "Harnden's got too much to do," was his favorite argument, "and you'd just better give your parcels to us. Just try Adams for once. Adams is a little the nicest man you ever did see, and we have all the facilities for doing your business right up to the handle. Come, let me set these bundles into my wagon, and I'll put'em through by daylight. Mr. Dinsmore, the partner in New York, is a Boston man (he was made for an express-man), and will see to the delivery of these things himself."

With Sam as a canvasser, and Harnden's business declining, the Adams establishment made extraordinary progress Instead of desk room, the exclusive use of large and handsome stores was procured. Prodigal displays were made in the way of gas-fixtures, horses, wagons, and office boys. A net-work of minor express routes was absorbed, and all new ones were bought out as soon as they had demonstrated their practicability. First the service was extended to Washington, then between Hartford and Springfield, and afterward throughout the State of Connecticut. Agencies were established at all large stations in South Carolina, Georgia, Alabama, Tennessee, and Louisiana. West, Southwest, and the North were included in the system by giant strides, and in 1850 the business had actually become so important that Adams and Co. arranged to send their money and small packages over the New York and New Haven Railway, paying the sum of seventeen hundred dollars a month for a small space occupied in the car of a fast train. Soon afterward the style of the firm was changed to the "Adams Express Company," and much additional capital was invested, which materially assisted the development of the system.

The California express opened a vein of new wealth, and added greatly to the company's reputation. But the source of its present vast wealth was the immense business during the war of the rebellion. It has been truthfully said that no person unconnected with the company could imagine the

ST. CHARLES STREET, NEW ORLEANS.

magnitude of its transactions while the States were in conflict. On the nearest and most remote fields the agents of the express were always found, venturing often where a picket-guard would hardly venture, collecting money, letters, and trophies from the soldiers for transmission to "the loved ones at home." Many a thrilling episode might be related of the vicissitudes and perils endured by the expressmen in conveying these articles from the Southern frontier to their destination in the North. Where the armies went they followed with the zeal and pertinacity of newspaper correspondents. No quarters were too hot for them, and neither the shots of the enemy nor the rebuffs of the commanders drove them away. Around bivouac fires in the stillness of Southern forests they were found waiting for the homeward-bound messages that were hastily scribbled on the torn fly-leaves of prayer-books, or even on scraps of newspapers. Many a time in the thick of a battle a faint voice called them to the side of a fallen soldier, with the blood oozing from a

CHESTNUT STREET, PHILADELPHIA.

AN ARMY EXPRESS OFFICE.

death-wound in his breast, and entreated them to remain a moment while he transferred to their care a letter or a locket addressed to a girl in the North. Many a time, too, they saw a noble fellow fall into an eternal sleep before he could finish his message. A romancist might gather suggestions for countless pathetic incidents from the experience of the ex-pressmen who followed the armies during the rebellion. One of the most melancholy duties these brave fellows had to execute was the transmission of the bodies of the slaughter-ed to their relatives and friends. The delivery at the home office often occasioned heart-breaking scenes, as "some-body's darling," wrapped in a coarse shroud, was presented to the woman who had kissed his handsome face good-by scarcely six months before.

But there was a humorous and joyous aspect to the battle-field express, as to most other concerns of men. It was a favorite habit of the "boys" to send home trophies in the form of "confiscated property." The trophies were of the most heterogeneous character, and sometimes put the express-men to more trouble than less accommodating ser-vants would have endured. A terrified and howling French poodle was once sent direct from camp to an Eastern farm-house, and, in fact, live stock was very often the form of memento, or, as Mrs. Partington would say, the *momentum*, of a battle. Jew's harps, Confederate money, old pipes, bro-ken sabres, fractured rifles, tobacco pouches, tarnished epaulets, smeared sashes, and like things, were the com-monest and the most portable of the mass forwarded. The habits of thrift in which some of the Down-Easters had been reared were manifested in the care with which old clothes were sent home after a new outfit had been supplied to the regiment. Thousands of boxes containing such worthless rags passed through the express consigned to remote vil-lages in Maine, Vermont, New Hampshire, and Northern New York. Full charges were collected for them, and when the expectant friends at home tore off the cover, it was only to find a ragged pair of trowsers and a coat. After a regiment had been paid off an immense number of money packages were intrusted to the express, and as the charges were high and the risks small, the profits of the company were magni-

LOADING UP IN THE GENERAL OFFICE AT NEW YORK.

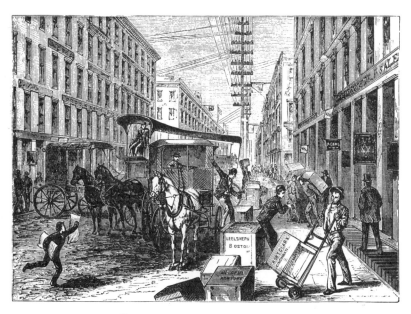

COLLECTION AND DELIVERY.

ficent. At one time the stock rose to the enormous price of five hundred dollars a share—the par value being one hundred. Thus had Alvin Adams's little venture with a dollar carpet-bag grown into a concern which made him and his partners millionaires.

After Harnden's death his emigration business was continued by Dexter Brigham, Jr., Robert Osgood, J. C. Kendall, and John W. Fenno. The New York and Boston Express, which had fallen into other hands in the mean time, retained its old name, and until 1860 it extended its branches almost as rapidly as the Adams; but it has since been merged into that concern, and is now a mere tributary. Harnden on his deathbed exclaimed that all he desired to live for was to see his foreign enterprise established on a permanent basis. Very soon after his interment the whole work fell to the ground. His successors were crippled by an unfortunate investment in a line of steam-ships, and failed for a very large amount.

The only formidable opponent of the Adams Express

Company existing at present is the American. Nearly all the other organizations are subordinate to these two, which are said to control the entire business. The growth of the American Express Company illustrates the pluck, energy, and perseverance of its founders, who were similar in these things to Adams and Harnden. In 1841 Henry Wells was agent of the latter at Albany, and urged his employer to penetrate the Western country with the express. Harnden made the answer that we have already quoted: "Put a people there, and my express shall follow." Wells was so confident, however, that the population was sufficiently numerous to support an express that he mentioned his idea to George Pomeroy, who was favorably impressed with it, and lost no time in putting it into effect. An express was accordingly started between Albany and Buffalo, Pomeroy acting as his own messenger, clerk, and boy, as Adams and Harnden had done before. But for some reason of which we are not informed he broke down after making three trips, and the business was suspended until Wells and Crawford Livingston offered to join him. Under the new firm the express was established upon an enduring foundation. A trip was made once a week, and occupied three days and four nights, which was the quickest time then on record. From Albany to Auburn the railroad was used, then the stage-coach, and afterward a private conveyance. Wells, who left Harnden, was appointed messenger, and while he acted in that capacity he never missed a trip. In the course of two years the traffic had so largely increased that daily trips were necessary, and a branch express was established between Albany and New York. But the business was still small, and could be accommodated in the trunk which Wells carried with him on the outside of the Buffalo coach.

One day, when the style of the firm had been changed to Livingston, Wells, and Co., Mr. Wells came into the office with a shrewd idea, which gave the concern an important impetus in its march toward prosperity. It was the year pre-

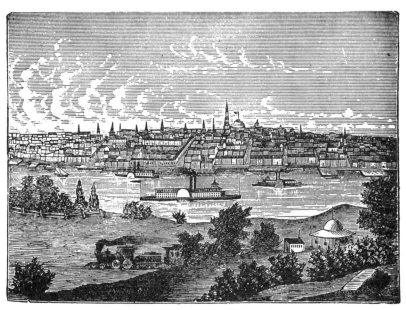

A VIEW OF ALBANY, NEW YORK.

vious to the reduction of letter postage by an act of Congress, and the Post-office was supporting some sixteen thousand politicians as postmasters by charging the outrageous price of twenty-five cents on every letter sent from Buffalo to New York. Wells's idea was to start an opposition, not in indignation meetings or in petitions, but in actual traffic. And in several columns of neat little figures he showed his partners how a letter could be carried for six cents at a handsome profit. It happened that those associated with Wells were just such clear-headed, enterprising fellows as himself, and they took hold of the project in a spirit of determination. When the express post-office was first opened, and stamps were sold at the rate of twenty for a dollar, the greatest interest was excited in the undertaking. Public meetings were called, and resolutions passed by the merchants and citizens generally not to send or receive letters by mail to or from any point included by the express until there was a reduction in the United States postage. Immense numbers of letters were sent through Livingstone,

Wells, and Co.'s hands, and the profits were greater than those derived from the conveyance of parcels. The government used every means to suppress the firm, and the messengers were arrested daily at the instance of the Post-office officials; but in every instance citizens stood ready with bail-bonds filled out and executed. Many stirring scenes were enacted. Officers were on the track at every point, and sometimes fierce affrays occurred. The expressman on horseback, with his mail-bag strapped across his broad shoulders, galloped many a hot mile across the rough coun-

WILLIAM G. FARGO.

PURSUIT OF EXPRESS MAIL CARRIER BY GOVERNMENT AGENTS.

try with a couple of angry pursuers at his heels. But the officers were discomfited throughout the strife, and after a futile contest with the opposition, the government began to think of looking for a remedy.

Mr. Wells, in behalf of himself and several wealthy merchants, offered to carry all the mail matter of the United States at an average rate of five cents per letter. The proposition was peremptorily rejected; but the opposition, in which James W. Hale had joined, was so resolute and so generally sustained by the people that during the next session of Congress a law was passed reducing the rate of postage three-fourths. As soon as the reform was accomplished, Hale, Wells, and others retired from the field, and again devoted themselves to the express.

In 1845 the firm of Livingston, Wells, and Co. had received a valuable acquisition in the services of William G. Fargo, who was chosen as a suitable man to extend the express into the country west of Buffalo, and Fargo did not disappoint his employers. He worked with extraordinary force, and in the course of a few years express wagons were traveling at regular intervals between the East, Cincinnati, Chicago, and St. Louis. Several changes occurred during the next few years in the style and the constituency of the original firm, and in 1850 it was represented by Wells and Co., Livingston and Fargo, and Butterfield, Wasson, and Co., who were opposed to each other. The principal of the latter firm was a man of wealth. He had been a stage-coach driver when a young man, and had risen to be owner of nearly all the stage lines running in Western New York. In 1849 he was engaged in transporting freight across the Isthmus of Panama. He was also projector of the Morse Telegraph line between Buffalo and New York, and he not only built it, but also put it into successful operation. Enlisting others with him, he founded a line of Lake Ontario and St. Lawrence steamers, and in 1849 he formed the express company of Butterfield, Wasson, and Co. We suppose he may claim to be founder of the American Express Company, for

EXPRESS WAGONS ON LAKE STREET, CHICAGO.

JOHN BUTTERFIELD.

in 1850 he approached Henry Wells with the acceptable proposition that the three firms should be consolidated under that title. No time was lost in consummating the necessary arrangements, and the Adams Express Company then found a rival which has advanced with it step by step, and is now one of the wealthiest corporations in America.

About a year later the celebrated California express of Wells, Fargo, and Co. was founded by several gentlemen connected with the American Company. Its growth exceeded that of the earlier expresses in brilliancy, and most of the local express lines were bought out in a short time. In 1857 $59,884,000 in gold were transported over their lines in California alone. Henry Wells, you will remember, started life as one of Harnden's messengers, and William G. Fargo rose from an equally humble position. If these glimpses of the history of the express system have no other merit, we may hope, at least, that they offer encouraging examples to the young.

"Overland to California in thirteen days." This was the next and greatest achievement of the express, and excited scarcely less interest than the Pacific Railroad itself. In 1858 or 1859 a company was formed in California under the name of the Central Overland California and Pike's Peak Express, a title fit to arrest the attention of the world. The president and the originator, we believe, was Mr. William H. Russell, and the stock-holders were mostly Californians. It was an audacious speculation, but it offered as many advantages to the mercantile community as the Atlantic cable and was hailed with as much satisfaction. No telegraph had linked the two oceans, and the stage-coach or the steamer

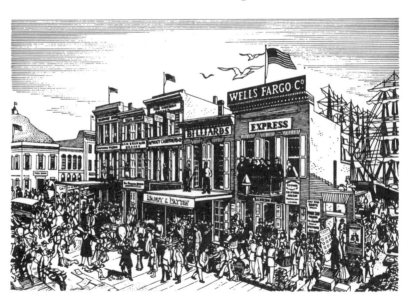

MONTGOMERY STREET, SAN FRANCISCO, IN 1852.

IN THE SIERRA NEVADA.

was the only vehicle by which a message or letter could be
sent. The new service consisted of a pony express, with stations sixty miles apart, across the continent. A large capital
was necessary, and the risks assumed were sufficient to
frighten away all but the daring Western speculators. The
rate fixed was five dollars in gold per quarter ounce, which,
of course, limited the matter carried to business letters. The
eastern terminus of the route was St. Joseph, Missouri, and
the western terminus Sacramento. From the latter town to
San Francisco the messengers traveled by steamboat, and
from St. Joseph to New York by railroad. The time occupied between ocean and ocean was fourteen days, and between St. Joseph and San Francisco ten days, as per the fol-
lowing time-table:

St. Joseph to Marysville .... 12 hours.

"	" Fort Kearney	34	"
"	" Laramie	80	"
"	" Fort Bridger	108	"
"	" Salt Lake	124	"
"	" Camp Floyd	128	"
"	" Carson City	188	"
"	" Placerville.................	226	"
"	" Sacramento	232	"
"	" San Francisco	240	"

The express was dispatched weekly from each side with not more than ten pounds of matter. The riders chosen were selected from plains-men, trappers, and scouts, familiar with the Indians, and capable of great bodily endurance. In consideration of the danger to which they were exposed, their salary was fixed at the enviable amount of $1200 a month each. The ponies were swift and strong, a cross in breed between the American horse and the Indian pony. Messengers and steeds were run sixty miles, and then awaited the arrival of the express from the opposite direction.

Such was the plan of the Central Overland California and Pike's Peak Express Company; and on a memorable day, the 3d of April, 1860, the first messenger was to start from St. Joseph. The *Daily Gazette* of that town issued a "Pony Express Extra" in honor of the occasion. It was a small single sheet, printed on one side only, and the first two columns were devoted to a heavily leaded account of the new enterprise, with this greeting to the press of California:

"Through the politeness of the express company we are permitted to forward by the first pony express the first and only newspaper which goes out, and which will be the first newspaper ever transmitted to California in eight days. The first pony will start at precisely five o'clock this afternoon, and letters will be received from all points up to 4.30. A special train

ST. JOSEPH, MISSOURI.

will be run over the Hannibal and St. Joseph Railroad for the purpose of bringing the through messenger from New York. The nature of the conveyance necessarily precludes our making up an edition of any considerable weight. It, however, contains a summary of the latest news received here by telegraph for some days past from all parts of the Union. We send in it greeting to our brethren of the press in California."

In a cloud of dust, and amidst the loud cheers of the population, the messenger galloped through the straggling streets on to the broad prairies reaching beyond the horizon. The route chosen was somewhat north of the present track of the Pacific Railroad. It lay, as the time-table shows, from St. Joseph to Laramie, thence up the Sweet Water to Salt Lake, and down the Humboldt to Sacramento. Night and day the express went forward at the greatest speed attainable with ordinary horseflesh. As soon as a station was reached, one messenger, without waiting to dismount, tossed his bag to another already mounted, who in a few minutes was out of sight in the direction of the next relay.

INDIANS ATTACKING AN

OVERLAND EXPRESS COACH.

So for eight days, with fresh horses and messengers every sixty miles, the ride was continued through the awful canons of the mother range, up the bowlder-strewn foothills, between forests of hemlock, pine, and fir, through hot little mining towns, until Sacramento was reached, scarcely a minute behind the prescribed time.

The pony express fulfilled its promises for two years. The messengers were often followed by hostile Indians, and several were killed. In addition to their letter-bag they only carried one revolver and a bowie-knife. They ran and fought at the same time, and many a red-skin kissed the dust in atonement for those messengers who were slaughtered.

At the end of two years, in 1862, the telegraph line across the continent had been completed, and there was no longer any use for the pony express. The company was dissolved, having lost $200,000 in its courageous enterprise.

The Central Overland was the only important pony express that maintained itself in America. Goods and passengers had been sent to California by stage-coaches, in the free use of which Wells, Fargo, and Co. extended their reputation, although they forwarded the bulk of the matter by steamer *via* the Isthmus. The Overland Mail Company was started in 1858, and contracted with the United States government to carry a monthly mail from San Francisco to the Missouri River in consideration of $650,000 paid anually. John Butterfield was president, associated with William G. Fargo, William B. Dinsmore, and others. The route chosen was known as the Ox Bow, and came East by the way of Santa Fé; but in 1860 the Indians were so troublesome that the route of the pony express was adopted. Opposition lines were started, and the mail was afterward sent daily, in consideration of $1,000,000 anually. Ultimately, however the firm of Wells, Fargo, and Co. bought out the entire business, and was changed into a corporation, with a capital of $15,000,000.

A mere summary of the adventures of the overland mail-

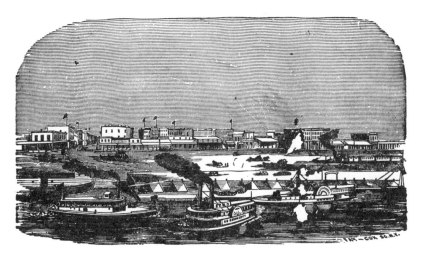

SACRAMENTO, CALIFORNIA, IN 1875.

coaches would more than fill the whole space allotted to us
We have before us, for instance, a curious pamphlet setting
forth the claims of Benjamin Holladay on the United States
government for loss suffered through the raids of Indians
during the time he was employed as a trans-continental
mail carrier. It contains fifty-nine large pages of terse affidavits, each describing an encounter with the savages, and
the best we can do, by the way of illustration, is to briefly
quote from three of them. In the first the affiant is Richard
Murray, a driver in the Territory of Utah:

*"Affiant states that he was passing from Split Rock
Station west to Three Crossings of Sweet Water with
the United States mails on the said 17th day of April,
A.D. 1862, in company with eight other men, all of
the mail party; that they were attacked by a band of
Indians numbering thirty or more, who commenced
a furious fire upon them with rifles and bows and arrows; that resistance was made by said mail party for
hours, when the Indians retreated. Affiant further
states that six men out of the nine who composed said
party were wounded, one with arrows and five with
guns."*

The second affiant from whom we shall quote is Lemuel Flowers, a district agent:

"*Affiant says that on the 17th of the same month [April, 1862] the Indians attacked a party of nine men running two coaches, and commenced a furious fire upon them, wounding six men, including this affiant, whose body was penetrated by two rifle-balls; that after a resistance of four hours the Indians captured nine head of mules, nine sets of harness, and partially destroyed two coaches.*"

The third affiant, who has the worst tale to tell, is George H. Carlyle:

"*On the 9th August, 1864, I left Alkali Station for Fort Kearney. On reaching Cottonwood Springs I learned by telegraph that the Indians had attacked a train of eleven wagons at Plum Creek, killed eleven men, captured one woman, and run off with the stock. Upon hearing this I started down the road, and when a few hundred yards off Gillman's Station I saw the bodies of three men lying on the ground, fearfully mutilated and full of arrows. At Plum Creek I saw the bodies of the eleven other men whom the Indians had murdered, and I helped to bury them. I also saw the fragments of the wagons still burning, and the dead body of another man, who was killed by the Indians at Smith's Ranch, and the ruins of the ranch, which had been burned.*"

The language of the affidavits is not dramatic, and the reader must use his imagination a little in order to realize the sufferings and heroism of those who traveled across the plains twelve years ago.

When the line *via* the Isthmus of Panama was started, the express matter was forwarded by through messengers from New York to San Francisco. The route was from the metropolis to Aspinwall, thence up the Chagres River, and

A MESSENGER OF THE PANAMA ISTHMUS SERVICE.

by portage to the Pacific. Immense wealth was entrusted to the messengers, among whom there were many picturesque characters—picturesque both in person and manners. They usually wore loose blue shirts, trowsers tucked into capacious boots, slouch hats, and numerous weapons of defense. They guarded their treasure with the utmost vigilance, and we believe never lost a single ounce of the tons of gold-dust which were at one time intrusted to them.

In 1852 another use was found for the express, in the transfer of the baggage of travelers from the railroads and steamboats to their residences. Warren Studley started the system in New York, with an office in Manhattan Alley. It abated the hackney-coach nuisance, and also proved to be very successful from a pecuniary point of view. Similar expresses were soon afterward established in all other large cities, and Studley's was absorbed by Mr. Dodd, who has made it one of the famous institutions of New York. Hiram Studley, a brother of Warren, was the first man to carry a passenger across the city in a transfer coach—another improvement and extension of the express system—and for

WELLS, FARGO & CO. HEADQUARTERS AT SAN FRANCISCO.

NASSAU STREET, NEW YORK.

several days he was in danger of assassination by the irate "cabbies," who foresaw the injury it would do their business.

We have now only to glance at the present "carpet-bag" of the Adams and American Express companies. A credible authority informs us that it is an ordinary occurrence for the Adams Express Company to carry merchandise and "valuables" worth twenty million dollars in a single day. The United States Treasury intrusts to it the carriage of all bank-notes and specie; and with the American it transacts a greater exchange and banking business by the transfer of money than all the private bankers put together. The dividends paid on the capital stock are enormous, and have made millionaires out of men who started with the express in the capacity of office boys and messengers. Scarcely forty years ago John Hoey was engaged by Alvin Adams as a small boy in general, and his duties consisted of running errands, pasting labels on merchandise, and so forth. The same boy is now one of the wealthy men of the metropolis, and until recently was an active superintendent of the concern. We might mention at least fifty similar instances. Mr. Adams remains at the head of the Boston office, giving the service his constant attention, assisted by his sons Waldo and Edwin.

The two great companies employ nearly eight thousand men, one thousand five hundred horses, twelve hundred wagons, and three thousand iron safes. They travel over a hundred thousand miles daily, or over thirty-two million miles yearly! Scarcely a railway train runs on any road that has not a special car attached devoted to the business of the express, and no inhabited part of the country has been left unpenetrated. Wherever there is a station and a few dozen people, there is also an express office which is in communication with a thousand others spread throughout the Union. The system extends as far north as Oregon, as far west as California, as far south as Texas, and as far east as Canada. It is the most important agent of communication between the producer and the consumer, and they could no more dispense with it than with the Post-office or the banks.

In all our streets, on all our wharves, the strong and handsome wagons of our express companies, drawn by powerful horses, are seen loaded high with merchandise on every working day. In order to understand the extent to which they are patronized, we have only to look at the large cards exhibited outside the warehouse doors, bearing on them the names of the different expresses — the United States, National, American, or Adams. Each wagon has a district which it perambulates three times a day for the purpose of collecting goods to be forwarded, and the card indicates which express is wanted. The bulkiest and the most delicate articles, jewelry and watches, mowing machines and steam-plows, are alike intrusted to the same vehicle and pass through the same careful hands. The extreme care bestowed upon all things is one of the chief reasons why the express is so popular. Sometimes there is occasion for fault-finding, to be sure, but considering the immense quantity of merchandise transported, it is surprising how little is damaged in transit. An accident which occurred to a valuable article in charge of an expressman is said to have given rise to one of our most classical expressions. A bonnet was forwarded from one of our city milliners to a lady in the country, and when the box was delivered, it was evident that some one had been attempting to walk through it. The expressman stammered an apology as he presented it to the lady. "Oh yes, I understand," the fair dame exclaimed; "you've put your foot into it, and that's what's the matter!"

The C. O. D. system of the express is one of the greatest conveniences ever conferred on the mercantile community,

PORTLAND, OREGON, IN 1865.

but it has been largely used by swindlers, who have found in it a ready means of alluring the foolish. The imitation-greenback-sawdust rascals have caught not a few verdant countrymen by the pretense of honesty in dealing which the C. O. D. plan affords.

One of the most stirring occasions in the routine of express duties is the sale by auction of the "old hoss," or unclaimed freight which accumulates from time to time. When every possible method to find the owners has been tried and failed, an auctioneer is called in and the articles are sold to defray expenses. No package is allowed to be opened or examined until it has been purchased, and a spirit of speculation is thus excited in those who assemble. Small carefully sealed packages bring the highest prices, on the supposition

UNCLAIMED PARCELS ARE SOLD AT AUCTION.

that they may contain jewelry. An avaricious old customer once paid ten dollars for a neat little brown paper parcel sealed with evident care at both ends. It contained a hundred or more "rejected addresses" from a swain to "the fair sun of all her sex." Another similar parcel was knocked down to a bidder for eight dollars, and was found to contain a set of false teeth. Patent medicines, whisky (a still more patent medicine), toys, old clothes, surgical instruments, disinfectants, preserved animals, old magazines, false hair, and many stranger things are usually found among the "old hoss" packages. It may be assumed that most of them are of small value, as we have said, inasmuch as either the sender or the consignee of valuables would take care to have a thorough search made for any valuable property.

Of the Coaches, Wagons, & Carriages

VIRTUALLY all means of transportation then available were used by the express companies, the common-denominator factors being optimum speed, economy and security. The "backbone" vehicle of the industry, however, was the horse-drawn carriage in its numerous and varied forms—all the way from the magnificent mail coach (popularly called "stage coach") to the unpretentious buggy.

The best and most serviceable of these were manufactured at Concord, New Hampshire, where, in the same year (1837) that William Harnden founded America's earliest express enterprise, Lewis Downing commenced building the line of carriages that ultimately became famed as the finest in the world.

Carriage-making during that mid-nineteenth-century period achieved a near-perfection of harmonious merging of superb craftsmanship and a high degree of esthetic responsibility. The industry combined a diversity of hand-working skills rarely encountered in one trade, embracing, as it did, the use of wood, iron, steel, brass, cloth, silk, leather, paints and oils, hair and sometimes glass, rubber and ivory. And the array of trained artisans employed at a first-class establishment was impressive: body-makers, who constructed the seating- or carrying-compartment or enclosure; carriage-makers who made, fitted and joined the numerous parts of the understructure; wheelwrights to form, fit and balance the wheels; several classes of smiths, to make tires, springs, wheel-parts and axletree parts, and for special work involved in strengthening the framework with long metal edge-plates; accomplished and talented "heraldry painters;" and upholsterers proficient in working with a wide range of covering and lining materials including patent leather.

Selection of materials was of paramount importance, requiring a remarkably intimate knowledge of inherent natural qualities of different woods and metals. For the basic framework of the body and understructure, ash was used : for the body, this had to be "full grown mild and free-nature ;" for the understructure, "strong and robust" was specified ; and for the carriage-poles "younger growth, straight and tough." It was stipulated that wooden planks where needed (from 1½″ to 6″ thick) must have been seasoned at least one year for each inch of thickness.

After the framework was completed, the body would be panelled with ¼″ "mild Honduras mahogany, plain and free from grain" and every joint carefully coated with ground white lead for waterproofing. Roofs of coaches were covered with either ¼″ white pine boards or boards specially cut from the circumference of the tree, five feet wide or more, in three thicknesses cross-grained and glued together under pressure.

The timber used for wheels was "wych elm for the naves [hubs], heart of oak or hickory for the spokes, and ash for the felloes [rims]." The felloes were frequently made in two sections, bent into a circle. All of these pieces were shaped, finished and assembled by hand.

When metal springs were used, the best were of steel, tapered at the ends of the leaves by hand at the anvil, for good elasticity. Abbot, Downing coaches had, instead of springs, two lengths of leather straps supporting the body. Called "thoroughbraces," these were made of multiple layers of heavy steer-hide, and they allowed the body to rock sideways as well as back and forth. Downing invented the thoroughbrace, and this feature contributed greatly to the success and popularity of Abbot, Downing's Concord Coach and California Mud Wagon. Interestingly, its purpose seems to have been principally to benefit the horses, for it was found that without the shock-absorbing thoroughbraces, the violent jolting sustained by heavily-loaded vehicles traveling fast over the rough roads soon ruined good teams.

At the best carriage-works, as many as twenty coats of

paint and varnish were applied, and it was recommended that after the first year of use, the brilliant gloss be restored by careful polishing "with rottenstone and oil." Road-lamps, handles and auxiliary furniture made of silver or brass were supplied by specialty manufacturers.

Interiors of closed coaches were often lined with fine tapestry cloth, embroidered fabric or morocco leather, and exterior panels were sometimes decorated with well-executed color paintings of landscape views, historic scenes or portraits of illustrious persons.

Modest utility wagons, as well as the splendid mail coaches, were often painted bright red, blue, green or black on the body, with ornamental tracery patterns or filigree designs in yellow or gold. Wheels and running-gear were usually a brilliant, sparkling yellow, and the leather-work was a rich black.

The prices charged by Abbot, Downing, converted to present-day (March, 1970) values based on the U. S. Government Gold Standard, would be about 1.69 times the figures given in their "Chart A" catalog of 1871. It is probably merely an academic exercise to attempt to translate values by this method, however. Indeed, it is doubtful that one of the full-dress stage coaches (no two of which, incidentally, were exactly alike) could be reproduced identically today for less than the price of a moderately comfortable three-bedroom suburban residence.

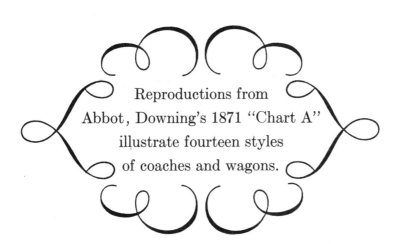

Reproductions from
Abbot, Downing's 1871 "Chart A"
illustrate fourteen styles
of coaches and wagons.

THE ABBOT, DOWNING COMPANY.

MANUFACTURERS of

COACHES & WAGONS,

Concord, N.H. USA.

Boston, Mass.   388-400 Atlantic Ave.

New York, N.Y.   1135 Broadway.

Chart A.

Entered according to act of Congress in the year 1871 by Abbot Downing & Co. in the Office of the Librarian of Congress at Washington

The use of our Coaches and Wagons on all the Mail routes in America and the English Colonies for many years is a guarantee of their superiority.

The use of our work in the Australian Colonies for the past sixty years is a guarantee of its excellence.

All our lumber is carefully seasoned to meet the requirements of a dry climate, and all parts, including wheels, axles and spring, being made within our works, of well-tested material, we are able to give to our customers Carriages which we know to be reliable.

The setting of the Axletrees gives to our Wagons an ease of draught not found in other vehicles.

We are prepared to manufacture any style of vehicle not on our charts that the fancy of the purchaser may dictate.

Parties ordering will be particular to name width of track, measuring from outside of one wheel to the inside of the other, on the ground.

THE MAIL COACH.

With leather boots both front and rear, leather apron, deck
seat (front), brake, road-lamps and ornamented sides.

To seat 12 inside . . . . $ 1,200
   "   9   "   (heavy)   1,100
   "   9   "   (medium)   1,050
To seat 6 inside, with either two
    seats for three on each side, or
    three seats for two on each side   1,000

Optional additions :
    For deck seat on rear   20
    For packing body only   12
    For packing coach complete   20

Optional deductions :
    If no road-lamps   7
    If no front deck seat   20
    If no ornamental paint   20

HACK PASSENGER WAGON, No. 209.*

With doors, top railing, leather-lined body, leather curtains, rear boot, leather driver's apron, brake & lamps.

To seat 9 inside . . . . $ 625
    " 6 "   550
    " 4 "   500
For seat on top and cushion, add   12
If open rack instead of rear boot, deduct .   20
If rear boot and flap tarpaulin, deduct . .   15
If curtains enamel duck, deduct   6

[*This was the "California Mud Wagon."]

OVERLAND WAGON, No. 201.

With doors, top covered with sail duck painted, sail duck or enameled curtains, lamps, brake, lined with leather, & rear boot and driver's apron leather.

To seat 9 inside . . . . $ 600

" 6 " 525

MAIL WAGON, No. 203.

With top covered with sail or enamel duck, leather lining,
rear boot and driver's apron of leather, lamps & brake.

To seat 9 inside . . . . $ 525
    " 6 " 475
If rear boot flap tarpaulin, deduct . . .   15
If driver's apron duck   7

MAIL JERKER, No. 212.

With brake, road lamps, rear rack, sail duck top, seats for 4. Hung on leather thoroughbraces . . . . $ 265

WAGON No. 3. ☛

With hickory wheels, steel tires, half patent axles, boot behind seat, rubber driver's apron, removeable front seat.

As shown . . . . $ 195
If leather apron, add 7
If no boot at rear, deduct 10
If top and curtains same as No. 2, add . . 110

Wagon No. 1.

With hickory wheels, steel tires, half patent axles, rubber driver's apron, leather or panel boot behind seat.

As shown	$ 165
If leather apron, add	7
If no boot at rear, deduct	10

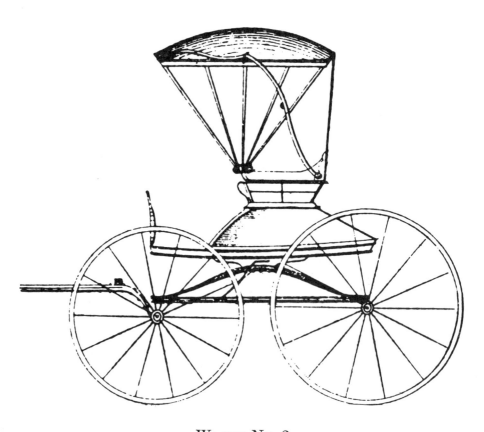

WAGON No. 2.

With top, cushion-back seats and curtain-sides attaching
to top, otherwise same as No. 1 . . . . $ 260

Optional additions to Nos. 1, 2 and 3:

For pole with shafts	$ 20
For pole, but no shafts	8
Brake.	15
Patent coupling for short turning	6
Packing for shipment (single carriage) . .	10
Packing two or more, per carriage . . .	6
Full-plated joints on tops	8
Front bonnet for tops	10
Full dash instead of center-plate	3

AMBULANCE WAGON, No. 205.

With doors, top covered with sail duck painted, curtains of sail or enamel duck. Hung on leather braces, or table springs and perches. Rear boot with tarpaulin flap, duck driver's apron.

To seat 9 in all . . . . $ 575
"   6   "   525

WAGON No. 17.

With hickory wheels, steel tires, half patent axles, cloth or
leather lined, as shown . . . . $ 375
(May be had with optional additions same as Nos.1, 2 & 3.)

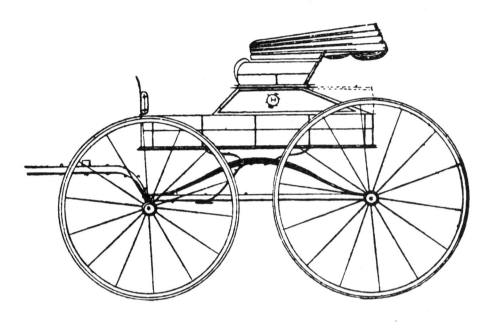

WAGON No. 24.

With hickory wheels, half patent axles, steel tires, rear
boot level or at slant, as shown . . . . $ 275
(May be had with optional additions same as Nos.1, 2 & 3.)

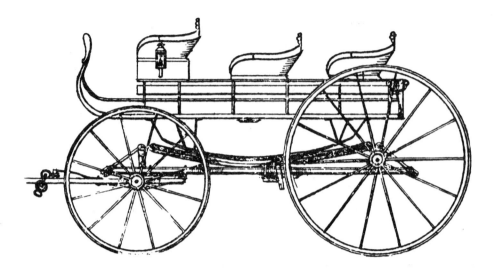

PICNIC WAGON, No. 208.

With brake, road-lamps, leather apron, tail board to drop down, hung on leather braces.

To seat 9 in all	$ 360
" 6 "	325
For light bow top over all, add	35
For rack behind, add	10
If no brake, deduct	15
If no lamps, deduct	6
If no apron, deduct	10

BEVERLY WAGON.

Upholstered in either leather, cloth or corduroy, with hickory wheels, steel tires, half patent axles and pole. As shown . . . . $ 290

    For rubber tires, add . . . . 35 to 40

    For road-lamps, add   15

    For shafts in addition to pole, add   . . .   15

OF THE ILLUSTRATIONS

THE ILLUSTRATIONS on these pages were reproduced from the August, 1875 issue of *Harper's New Monthly Magazine*, from prints loaned by the Wells, Fargo Bank, and from materials in the publisher's collection.

The Wells, Fargo Bank History Room at San Francisco graciously made available their copy of the Abbot, Downing Co. "Chart A" catalog for 1871, for the pictures of carriages; the map of western stage and express routes (back endpapers), and the picture "Montgomery Street, San Francisco in 1852" (page 36).

Unfortunately little is known of the identity of the artist creators of the drawings. Only one picture ("Auction Scene", page 50, initialled "C. S. R.") by C. S. Reinhart, is positively identified. "View of Omaha in 1875" on page 21, and "Sacramento in 1875" on page 43, apparently were engraved by the firm of Fay-Cox, since their names appear in the lower right, where engravers traditionally identified themselves. Often, they would add "sc" (for the Latin *sculpsit*: engraved it). Artists usually signed at the lower left, frequently adding "del" (for *delineavit*: drew it). The "Lake Street, Chicago" picture on page 34 is assumed to have been engraved by Van Ingen and Snyder, on the same basis. All three of these illustrations may well have been engraved after standard anonymous originals, perhaps lettersheets, or possibly contemporaneous photographs.

The drawing of the post-boy and horse on the title page is a stock cut from a nineteenth-century printer's type specimen book.

COLOPHON

THIS book was designed by the publisher, printed at Ashland, Oregon, and bound at Filmer Brothers Press at San Francisco, California. The typeface for the text, headings and captions is Monotype Modern Roman, composed in England by Yendall & Company, Limited. The display typeface for the title page is American Type Founders' Caslon No. 471, and that for the folios is their Bank Script; both were hand-set. The paper is Curtis Utopian Text. The cloth is Columbia Mills' hopsacking.